Ministry of Connections

Jeremy Garlock, MA

Copyright © 2018 Jeremy Garlock

All rights reserved. No part of this publication may be reproduced, stored in a retrieval system, or transmitted, in any form or by any means, electronic, mechanical, photocopying, recording, or otherwise, without the prior written permission of the author.

Eaton Press

Published and Distributed by Eaton Press
EatonPress.com

"Always pray to have eyes that see the best in people, a heart that forgives the worst, a mind that forgets the bad, and a soul that never loses faith in God."

- Author Unknown

Contents

Introduction	1
Part 1: Connection Is Different For Everyone	4
Theory of Multiple Intelligences	5
Spiritual Intelligences	11
Stages of Human Development	15
Part 2: Connection Happens in Three Areas	23
• Fellowship (Controlled Hang Time)	24
• Service (Not Just Physical)	28
• Meaningful, Rigorous Bible Study	32
Part 3: Connection Happens More Than One Day A Week	36
• Ministry of Presence	37
• Ministry of Recognition	41
• Ministry of Discipleship	44
Part 4: Connecting From the Pulpit:	47
• Ideas To Help People Connect With	48
Part 5: Pulling It All Together	52
• Discipleship Jesus' Way	53
Appendices	
A. Suggestions For Using Multiple Intelligences In Your Ministry For Connecting Individuals To Your Teachings	57
B. Suggestions For Using Spiritual Intelligences For Connecting With God	61
C. Suggestion For Using Erikson's Theory of Human Development To Create	63
D. Fellowship Activities	66
E. Service Activities	68

F. Bible Study Ideas And Resources	**70**
G. Training Your Ministry Team For Connections	**76**
H. Model Sermon Format	**78**

Introduction

I get to speak with pastors and church leaders often about church health and church growth, and I have noticed a pattern in most of these conversations; they are usually conversations of statements. We leaders like to make statements like:

My church attendance is way down from what it used to be.

Our evangelistic events just don't bring people in like we want them to.

In our church, 20% of the people do 80% of the work.

Pew warmers! Our members are just pew warmers! They want the pastor to do all the work!

I'm frustrated.

I am not putting down these statements, and I'm not suggesting that they're wrong. Most likely they are 100% on point. The problem is that recognizing these facts will not lead us any closer to a solution. We need to cease conversations of statements and begin conversations of questions.

Why is church attendance way down?

Why don't people come to our events?

Why are so few people in our church participating in the work?

What is my church's greatest need?

In my experience, that last question is the question that every pastor and church leader should be asking themselves. Often we try to run programs in our churches without addressing the needs of our churches. But the church is like a person (it is a body after all!); as long as a church's needs are not being met that church cannot be healthy. As long as a church is not healthy that church will not have sustainable growth and the greatest need of any church is connection.

You see, God designed humans to be connected, and, therefore, God intended that the church be involved in a ministry of connections. The church should help people connect in the following ways:

- **Believers should be connected to God.** *"I am the vine; you are the branches. If you remain in me and I in you, you will bear much fruit; apart from me you can do nothing. If you do not remain in me, you are like a branch that is thrown away and withers; such branches are picked up, thrown into the fire and burned. If you remain in me and my words remain in you, ask whatever you wish, and it will be done for you. This is to my Father's glory, that you bear much fruit, showing yourselves to be my disciples." (John 15:5-8).*
- **Believers should be connected to each other.** *"They devoted themselves…to the fellowship…All the believers were together and had everything in common. Selling their possessions and goods, they gave to anyone as he had need. Every day they continued to meet together in the temple courts. They broke bread in their hoes and ate together with glad and sincere hearts…" (Acts 2:42-46).*
- **Believers should be connected to their leaders.** *"They devoted themselves to the apostles teaching…" (Acts 2:42).*
- **Believers should be connected to their church body.** *"The body is a unit, though it is made up of many parts; and though all its parts are many, they form one body. And so it is with Christ…Now you are the body of Christ, and each of you is a part of it." (1 Corinthians 12: 12, 27).*
- **Believers should be passionate about connecting to unbelievers.** *"…enjoying the favor of all the people. And the Lord added to their numbers daily those who were being saved. (Acts 2:46-47).*

Because this about being connected to God, believers, and others, I am taking for granted that you are a church leader who is involved in intense prayer and Bible study as you seek God's will. I am also taking for granted that you are leading your people to do the same. If you are not, please put this book down now and become such a leader. While the information here is good, it is nothing if it is not led by God's will and soaked in God's power and authority.

Church health and church growth are not about using the latest methods or gimmicks, and it's not about following the right formula. It is about connection, and when people are connected in these ways, there is an automatic increase in attendance and participation. Despite a lack of gimmicks, a church that is connected will turn into a church that is healthy, and a church that is healthy will be a church that is growing.

The contents of this book are not intended to be a formula or a gimmick or a method. This book is about answering the question, "What is my church's greatest need?" Ideas will be presented, but all of the ideas must be flexible, moldable, and absolutely not locked in iron. As you read, ask yourself another important question: "What am I learning that I can use to help my church be a church that participates in a ministry of connection?" If you can learn and apply that, then you will be well on your way to helping your church be a healthy and growing church.

One final note; because a ministry of connections is about making a church or a ministry healthy, and because it is not relying on gimmicks, the ideas behind it can work with any ministry. Small church, large church, children's church, youth ministry, young adult ministry, church schools, and other ministries all operate on the same underlying concepts. The key will be to take the ideas found in this book and apply it to the ministry that is within your sphere of influence.

PART 1

Connection Is Different For Everyone

We all learn differently. We all see life from different points of view. Where we are in life developmentally often dictates what are the "big things" we are dealing with. In short, connection is different for everyone. That is why cookie-cutter churches and ministries will, by nature, not connect with many individuals.

The Theory of Multiple Intelligences

Let's play a game. I have three mystery men in mind. I will give you some clues to each, and you see if you can guess who they are. Ready?

Mystery Man #1
- Famous Actor
- Born in Syracuse, NY
- Was a wrestler in high school
- Dyslexic

Do you know who this is? If you said the man is Tom Cruise, then you are correct.

Mystery Man #2
- Named his first two children Dash and Dot after the old telegram technology
- Did not like bathing, and went several days without cleaning up
- He invented the earliest tattoo machine
- He was removed from school after only three months of education because his teacher said he was uneducable.

Do you know who this is? If you said the man is Thomas Edison, then you are correct.

Mystery Man #3
- An accomplished violinist
- Didn't like to wear socks
- His brain was stolen
- An average student
- He flunked math

Do you know who this is? If you said the man is Tom Cruise, then you are correct.
Now, here is the real question. Did you notice a common theme

in these three mystery men? They are, or were, all wildly successful, yet would have been classified as unsuccessful by typical education standards. The main goal of education is to help individuals connect with learning, and then use that learning to connect to the world, shaping their minds and character in the process. It was thought for many years that a student's success both in education and in life could be predicted by a traditional IQ test. However, each of our mystery men lacked at least one natural ability needed to perform well on an IQ test, and in school. Tom Cruise lacked certain linguistic abilities, Albert Einstein lacked certain mathematical abilities, and Thomas Edison, well, he lacked the ability to sit still and focus. An IQ test may or may not have correctly predicted the school success rate of these men, but it could not predict their success in life. Why is that?

In the 1980's a new theory started to gain popularity in education circles based on the radical idea (yes, read some sarcasm there) that people learn differently and can have strengths that don't show up on an IQ test. This theory, published by psychologist Howard Gardner, is called the Theory of Multiple Intelligences. This theory's main idea is that every person has some combination of nine learning strengths or intelligences that help him or her connect to some sort of learning goal. The nine intelligences are as follows:

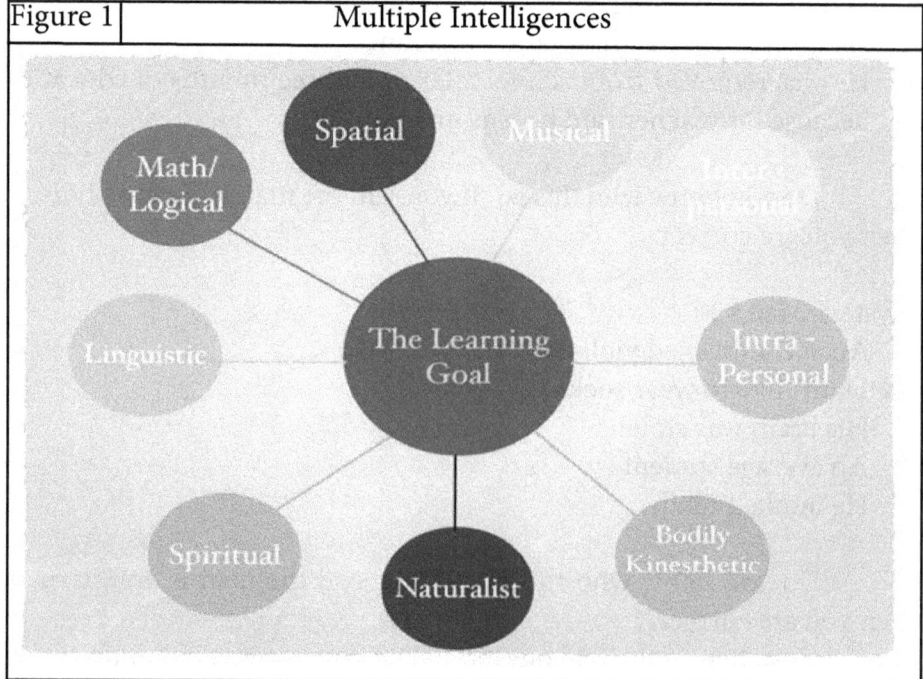

Figure 1 | Multiple Intelligences

1. **Spatial** – The ability to connect to the world and see how things physically go together and relate. This is why Thomas Edison couldn't learn in school but learned an awful lot about life by taking things apart and seeing how they go back together. My wife is strong at this. She can walk by a 1000 piece puzzle, pick up a puzzle piece and place it almost immediately. I do not have this. I look at the puzzle piece, compare it to the box for hours (literally) and put it down in frustration (resetting the urge to throw the box across the room) to go pick up my guitar.
2. **Musical** – The ability to connect to the world through music. I have this. I serenade my wife while she works on the puzzle. When I hear music, I am automatically analyzing the harmonies and the structure of the instrumentation. Since my brain is working overtime with music, I tend to remember things that are happening around me when the music is going. I learn through rhythm and connecting memories to melodies.
3. **Interpersonal** – This is the ability to connect to the world through our interaction with other people. People with this intelligence like to do group work because they learn and think as they think things out. They enjoy creating the synergy that happens in a good group. As a teacher, I used to get aggravated by those students who couldn't be quite and work. Then I realized that I am a person that needs to talk things out with someone else before I "get it." I decided to give my students the benefit of the doubt and let them talk it out when it came to their work. I came to find that, most of the time, they did drastically better on their assignments as a result.
4. **Intrapersonal** – This is the ability to connect to the world by first connecting to one's thoughts. These are your "journalers," and those that like to have some solitude to think out their thoughts. Often they come up with very profound ideas and connections. Many teachers have some type of escape place or a quiet place in their classroom. I have seen many a student go to these to get away from everyone else. You think they are there zoning out, but they often come back having heard and processed more than those than those that were right in front of you.
5. **Bodily-Kinesthetic** – This is the ability to connect to the world through physical movement. The most common example is the athlete, but, as a teacher, I've had numerous students who learned through hand motion and bodily movement.
6. **Naturalist** – This is the ability to connect to the world through nature. My mother-in-law has this strength. When she looks at a leaf, she

will begin to tell you about the types of vein patterns and the animals that like to eat it and how it is a part of an ecosystem. I will tell you it is green.

7. **Spiritual** – To be fair, Gardner calls this the existential intelligence, but since we are dealing with Christians, I will call it the spiritual intelligence. This is the ability to connect to the world by first making connections to the spiritual reality. This is that person in your Bible study who is always making connections to the spiritual with every movie they see, book they read, conversation they have, and circumstance they experience. The rest of us look on with a smile while thinking, "How did you see that?"

8. **Linguistic** – This is the ability to connect to the world through the written and spoken word. Novelists, essayists, journalists, pastors, and teachers are generally strong in this area. Some of us ain't speaking good enough English to qualify.

9. **Mathematical/Logical** – The ability to connect to the world through numbers and logic. In high 9school, I bemoaned the fact that this one passed me by.

Please notice an important point. It's not that people just enjoy these different intelligences, but they actually learn and connect to the world through them. We need to stay focused on the learning and connecting peace, and not get distracted by the idea that these are just different ways people have fun. In the "Practical Application" section below I will touch on some ideas of how to use multiple intelligences to enhance your ministry. Realize that this is more than letting people relax and enjoy themselves. This is about helping them connect with God, with each other, and learn.

You may be asking, "What does this have to do with church and having a ministry of connections?" Glad you asked! Think of the typical church service or Bible study you attend. What intelligences are normally used? Linguistic, spiritual, and maybe music and interpersonal. However, in many churches, the music, and interpersonal intelligences are downplayed, or at least not used to their fullest extent. That means that the service or Bible study is built to connect to roughly 3/9 of people who it may be trying to reach. Did you catch that? Typical methods are actually designed to disconnect from 6/9 of the people who need to be connected to Jesus Christ. That's over half the population! This, my friends, is not healthy.

The very first thing I recommend any ministry do (after praying, of course), whether working with young or old, whether working with small groups, individuals, or a large congregation, is to analyze what intelligences they are using, and how they can incorporate more of them into their services and weekly activities. Remember, the name of the game is to connect. So we need to begin by trying to structure how we do things in a way that will connect with the way people are naturally wired. You never know, you may have a version of an "uneducable" Thomas Edison in your pew, and they're not connecting with anything you're doing or saying. Don't be satisfied with that disconnection. Who knows? If you reach them, they may be a great man or woman for God!

Practical Application

My church is the Baldwinsville Adventist Church in Baldwinsville, New York. We call it B.A.C. for short. This church began as a small group consisting of three families that eventually grew into our current church, and it is still growing. It has grown because it is a church that has "accidentally" discovered the power of having a ministry of connection. Throughout this book, I will be sharing what we are doing at B.A.C., and sometimes in other ministries so that you can have an idea of how to use the ideas of this book practically.

When we were in our small group stage our services went about like this:

- We spent a lot of time, and I mean a lot of time in fellowship and eating (interpersonal intelligence). This time alone may last two hours.
- We then had an extended music service that lasted about a half hour, focusing on kid-friendly songs with motions (musical and bodily-kinesthetic intelligences).
- We then discussed as we read through a portion of the Bible (linguistic and spiritual intelligences). This was kept very interactive (interpersonal intelligence again), and we tended to focus on the practical meaning for our lives, leaving time for reflection (intrapersonal intelligence).
- We then went back to fellowship and activities (interpersonal and bodily-kinesthetic) and found that the conversations often continued on what we had just discussed (interpersonal and spiritual intelligences).

This was not rocket science, but it did create connections through intelligences (seven of them to be exact!) that aren't all used in a typical church service. When we decided to become a church we intentionally began to plan and experiment on how we could keep the same "feel" we had as a small group. Different adjectives were used to describe this "feel," but the best way I can describe it is a feeling of connection, with each other and with God. Elements of our church service still use many of the intelligences not often seen in a typical church service. For example we:

- Have an extended song service, with songs that are chosen to support the theme of the messaged preached (musical intelligence). It should be noted that the best sound equipment and musicians are used, and they practice often.
- The sermon is short and to the point, and interactive, with plenty of give-and-take between the congregation and the speaker (interpersonal intelligence).
- The sermon is still very Bible-based, and we delve into the Word (linguistic and spiritual intelligences).
- The sermon is still centered on how the truth of the Bible makes a practical impact on our lives, especially in our healing, with time for reflection (spiritual and intrapersonal intelligences).
- Presentation software, such as PowerPoint or Keynote, are often used to prove a point for those that are more visual than auditory (spatial intelligence). Please see the section on proper usage of presentation software in Part 4 to learn what to do and what not to do with this type of tool.
- The design of our church has a balcony wrapping around the worship area. This balcony contains the kitchen and fellowship area. During the sermon it is typical for many people, those that can't sit still, to be up there, preparing the food and tables for lunch (bodily-kinesthetic intelligence). Don't be fooled; they are not distracted. They are often leaning over the balcony to interact with the speaker.
- We still have a very long potluck lunch, lasting a few hours (interpersonal). And the cool thing is, people want to stay that long. It has been described as being like Thanksgiving every week.

Notice we have an unusual format, but the truth is preached using seven different intelligences. They say the proof is in the pudding, and our pudding consists of more and more people visiting our church and staying, becoming a part of a connected family.

For further ideas on how to use multiple intelligences at your church see Appendix A.

Spiritual Intelligences

"I've tried so hard!" she cried between the sobs and the tears. "I read my Bible every day. I pray and try to listen. But I just feel so disconnected from God. What's wrong with me?"
Some of you readers can immediately identify with this hurting young lady that my wife and I were counseling. You've been told that good Christians read their Bibles (which is true) and pray (again, this is true) and listen (which is true yet again), go to church (absolutely!) and that this is God's chosen method for connecting with His children (is that true?). The only thing is that no matter how much you participate in these activities you don't feel connected. Others of feel so close to God in prayer and Bible study and church attendance that this seems like heresy. What's the deal here?

"Kristin," (not her real name), "tell me about a time you did feel close to God."

"Ummm…." (much silent thought). "When I sing in choir I feel close to Him. When I sing at vespers, I feel close to Him. I guess when I'm singing."

"Then find every way you can to sing to God. At church, in the shower, in the car, when you walk to class. Every opportunity you get, sing! Oh, and, um, don't forget to read your Bible and pray too."
A few weeks later Kristin told me she was feeling closer to God than she had in such a long time. And, low and behold, her Bible reading and prayer times were also becoming more productive.

If I stopped the story there, it would seem that we were simply talking about multiple intelligences. That is obviously where we started. Kristin is extremely musical, and her musical intelligence was beginning to make connections for her other weaker intelligences. But the story doesn't stop there.

This conversation took place in Kristin's senior year of high school. The next year she was in college. As we all expected, Kristin gravitated to a musical major and musical extracurricular activities. But she also became active in service groups. She was always serving. Sometimes with music, sometimes with physical labor, and sometimes through various emotional support ministries. The next time we spoke,

Kristen told me that when she is in service for others, she feels very connected with God.

Again, some of you are nodding your heads. You love service. If only a church service were really a service! You could do it all the time and feel very connected to God. And, again, some of you are shaking your heads. I mean, come on, service is nice and all, but it doesn't take the place of a good Bible study and prayer session. And some of you are shaking your heads at both of these because yet something else connects you to God better than either of these.

I believe the answer lies in Luke 10:27. "He answered, 'Love the Lord your God with all your heart and with all your soul and with all your strength and with all your mind.'" Did you see all the ways of loving God here? Let's look again. "He answered, 'Love the Lord your God with all your heart and with all your soul and with all your strength and with all your mind.'" I believe wrapped up in this little verse another layer of multiple intelligences. Specifically, here are the four layers of spiritual intelligence. While all the multiple intelligences can help us connect to the world through learning, spiritual intelligence is the very intelligence needed to connect to God. Let's unwrap each layer of the spiritual intelligence.

With All Your Mind

Let me work the list backward because this is the very layer of the intelligence we Christians normally work with. There are those of us who love to think on the Word of God. We read it, try to become scholars, reading reference material, debating in our minds (or with others) over the different elements of truth. This is necessary, and it is good, and it is God's design for there to always be people who connect with God this way for their own benefit, and for spreading the truth of the gospel. But, it is not God's design for every person to rely on this to be their main mode of connection. Their main mode of identifying truth? Yes. But connection? Only for some.

With All You Strength

Let me introduce you to the Kristin's of the world. These are the people who love to be in service. That service might be in music, or in the church office, or by doing community service, or by going on mission trips, or by doing anything that is doing. It might be physical; it might not be. But, whatever it is, it is a service to glorify God, help people, and add to the kingdom. They may read their Bible (they should!). But their mode of connection, the point in which the feel the most alive with Jesus is when they are working for Him.

With All Your Heart

Some of us cry when we hear songs, or hear a powerful message that was just for us, or when we see beauty in the world. We laugh easily, and we love easily, and we hurt easily. And that connection with God somehow always triggers our emotions. I'm not saying we leave out logic, that we don't search the Scriptures to find the truth, or that we use our emotions alone to make all decisions and just do "what feels right." No, that kind of faith is a faith that is in error. But we do have powerful emotional responses. There is a connection there. And to try to have a Christian experience without it is to deny the passion with which God made us, and which He demonstrates towards us Himself.

With All Your Soul

Ever meet someone who just breathes their faith? It just comes out of their pores and is seen in all they do. While our faith does (or at leas should) be a central factor in how we live and the decisions we make, some people just have some sort of edge that the rest of us don't. They are the ones that have random people come up to them and say for no apparent reason, "You're a Christian, aren't you?" Again, they have elements of the other layers, but this is something beyond. It is a different kind of connection.

If you as a church leader, especially a leader with young people, then you need to help your people to understand that there is not one way to be spiritually smart. Not only that, but you need to help them discover which layer is their best avenue of connection, and then help them explore that layer. If you do this right, you will find that people will develop closer and deeper connections with Jesus. Like Kristin, they will go from "What's wrong with me?" to "I love this!"

Practical Applications

At B.A.C. the method that we, quite accidentally, learned worked for us was putting different people with different layers of spiritual intelligences in every aspect of our ministry. If you go to the adult class, you will see the lesson being taught by a great thinker, with passionate people sometimes openly moved to tears or at least talking passionately and opening their hearts. Others are making practical suggestions about what we can do in light of what's being shared, and still, others are there pulling it all together and loving on people the way Jesus would. How did we get to this point? We did this in four ways.

First, we openly welcome all different people in. We don't just avoid the pretension that a certain mold of Christian is what we expect and want to hear from; we openly teach that differences are welcome. This may mean getting away from the standard adult class material. At one point we were studying the book of John with the rule, "You can only talk about what you don't know." This opened up the way for the non-traditional Christians among us to shine.

Second, we purposely placed leaders who had strengths in the different layers in all areas. The people in the class I mentioned above are the regulars who are "assigned" to that room. Others come and go, but no matter who comes they will see someone who connects to God in a similar way as them and get the message they can connect, even if they are not in a particular mode. Our music team has a similar setup, though it was not done purposefully. There is a thinker/analyzer, there is a person who is always serving (more than one person, actually), there is at least one emotionally charged person on the team, and at least one person who just breathes their faith. And it comes out in the music service every week.

Third, we developed a simple but powerful church mission. This book is not about developing a mission. There are other great books on that. But it should be noted that we have a great one. "By the power of the Holy Spirit, broken people will be healed within our walls and without." Our whole mission is healing, and that means psychological, emotional, and social healing in addition to physical and spiritual healing. So we are very aware that how we function and relate to people will have a positive or negative psychological, emotional, social, and spiritual impact. So we better have our act together.

Lastly, we preach this from the pulpit. People who come will hear the straight truths of the Bible, but they also learn and are directly encouraged from the pulpit to explore God through different avenues. They are taught the importance of comparing everything with the Bible, which is the authority on God and His Truth. But they have the direct permission to explore alternate avenues of connection with God.

For further ideas of how to use layers of spiritual intelligence in your ministry see Appendix B.

Stages of Human Development

"The church is totally irrelevant to my life."

These are the words of a young adult to a fellow youth minister. And not just any young adult. She was raised in a good, Christian household. She attended Christian schools from kindergarten through college. She was a faithful member church youth groups. She was a camp counselor and girls' director at a Christian camp. And she is not alone. More and more young people and older people for that matter are telling us that the church is irrelevant to their life. What does this mean? It means the church is not connecting with their needs.

Often we think that everyone has the same needs. We think that everyone needs love, or respect, or clear truth, or interactive service. All of these things are important and have their place, but they do not help to connect with people where they are developmentally ready to be connected.

Psychologists have long known that at different times in our lives we humans have very specific needs. In the 1950's psychologist, Erick Erikson developed his Stages of Human Development, which emphasizes that we have different needs depending on the phase of life we are in.

Figure 2

Erick Erickson's Theory of Human Development

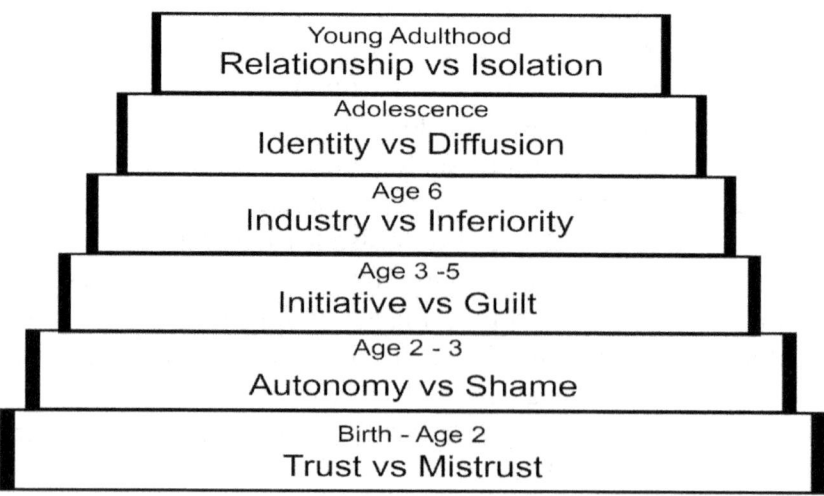

If you are a psychologist, you know this theory can go deep in both theoretical and practical terms. There are lessons pastors can learn regarding how to help their members have some healing by guiding them through these stages. But here in this chapter, we will focus only on how this theory can help our members connect to the church that they find so irrelevant.

Let me ask you a question. Are the ministries in your church designed to help to help your young people deal with the very issues that they are facing in their lives? And I'm not talking about drugs and sex and friends and choices. Those are subtopics. I'm asking if you are helping them learn to trust, have autonomy, become people of initiative, teaching them to be industrious, guiding them learn what their identity is, and then helping them make great relationships?

This is new ground for many churches. We have grown used to the idea of being different from "the world" and making our message focus on that difference. But, no matter how different we are supposed to be we are still humans, dealing with the same developmental needs as all other humans. If we don't connect with people with these needs, then we will continue to be irrelevant.

I would like to note that in his book They're Already Gone (2009), Beemer, Ham, and Hillard make the case that those young adults who leave the church when they go off to college actually "left" well before that. Because their needs were not met by the church most of them made the choice to leave in middle school and high school, and simply played along to appease their parents until that time. I say we need to meet those needs starting at the earliest stages possible, and continue to meet their varying needs throughout their lives.

Trust vs. Mistrust

At the very earliest ages, children are learning to either trust the world or not. Do mom and dad come to rescue them when they cry? If they have a need can they trust those over them to fill that need? Children who don't learn this become adults who can't trust people or God. So, while this seems like a non-spiritual issue, it cuts to the root of our spirituality. We need to have the trust of a child.

What does your church do to help these little ones (or older, distrustful ones) trust God? Do you give parenting classes to help parents and caregivers care for their young ones? Do you build a trusting, safe environment for your young ones where it is safe for them to make noise, make messes, and be little ones? For the older ones, do you act with integrity?

Autonomy vs. Shame

During this time young children are trying to be like the bigger people in their life. If you are cooking, they want to cook. If you are cleaning, they want to clean. If you are changing the breaks on the car, they want to change the breaks on the car. And though we all know it is easier to do these things without their "help," turning them away at this point will produce a sense of guilt in them. When we see them picking up the hammer to bang in nails along with us, and we respond by taking the hammer and saying in a stern voice, "That is for daddy!" we give them the impression that they should be ashamed of themselves. They're not good enough. And they may carry that around into adulthood, always feeling a sense of shame. It is so much better to find a way to include them in our activities, so they can properly learn to be autonomous children.

What does your church do to help these little ones (or older shame-filled ones) realize they are good enough to work for God, and that God wants their service just as much as He wants an adult's? Do you let them follow the deacons or deaconesses around and help them? To they get to help their teachers? Do they come to the church cleaning bees and lend a hand? Do they go visiting people with the elders (when appropriate, of course)? Do they help pick up the offering? Or are they asked to just sit and be still and passively take in the experience? If that's the case, they will lose interest very quickly.

Initiative vs. Guilt

The difference between this stage and the previous one is that now your little ones are not trying to be like you by doing things with you, but now they are taking the initiative to do things without you. They may try to make their cereal in the morning while you're still sleeping. You may walk into the bathroom to find them covered in your favorite lipstick. You may go out to the yard or garage to find your tools everywhere while they are building their latest project. How do you respond? Do you respond in a way that affirms their wonderful initiative while setting appropriate boundaries and responsibilities? Or do you get upset with them for having messed up your stuff? If you do that regularly, they may develop a guild complex that may last a lifetime.

What does your church do to help these little ones (or older guilt-laden ones) learn how to be wonderful people of initiative? Do you give them a position in the church and let them decide how they are going to fulfill their jobs? Do you tell them regularly that your door is always open to them if they need anything, and then stand by that promise? Do you praise, from the pulpit, those that take the initiative to do something? Or are people made to feel guilty or wrong because they tried something new? If that's the case, they will stop coming. They will go where they feel it is safe to learn initiative.

Industry vs. Inferiority

In this stage, young people need to learn that it is important to work hard, that they are better than others at something, and that it is ok to not be as good at something when compared to others. This is a healthy balance. Being a musician is important to me. Being a quality musician is very important to me. I needed to learn to practice hard and regular. I had a goal of being better than anyone else in my school as a guitarist. I may not have ever accomplished that goal, but I felt it was possible and worked at it. At the same time, I regularly met other guitarists and musicians that blew me away. It was important to come to grips that others can be better than me, and that is ok. We all may be a winner in God's eyes, but we are not all winners at everything all the time. This is a healthy perspective. The opposite is developing an inferiority complex. We weren't good enough to even try, or we just know that they are better than us and we get angry or deflated as a result.

What does your church do to help these young people (or older ones with inferiority complexes) learn to be industrious? Do ministry leaders, even young people who are asked to be part of your team, get treated based on the quality of work they do? This seems counter-intuitive because we want everyone to be loved, and that is true. But we sometimes put people in positions or keep them in positions based on popularity or fear of hurting them. They should be there based on performance. If I can't show up for music practice and if I continually play the wrong notes, then, no matter how good of a guitarist I may think I am, I should be removed from the music team.

Identity vs. Diffusion

Teenagers do stupid things. If you are offended by the idea that teenagers do stupid things, and if your memory is so short that you don't remember being a teenager, then ask auto insurance companies why it cost so much insure your teenager. Why do they do stupid things? They are trying to figure out who they are. For years they have grown up in your house learning what it means to be your child. Now they have to determine what it means to be a person separate from being your child. They will all of a sudden want to experiment with different foods (and no longer like the things they loved for years), experiment with different friends, experiment with different behaviors, and experiment with their faith. In healthy situations, the young person you raised will "disappear" for a few years and be replaced with a doppelganger that may look like them, but is definitely from a different universe, and then will reappear years later in a more mature form. In less healthy situations that doppelganger may be here to stay. What defines a healthy situation? The ability of the adults in their lives to let them experiment seems to be an indicator for if they will come to grips with their identity and return.

This experimentation must be within bounds. You don't want to encourage illegal drug use or a premarital sex life. But, if they are not allowed, for example, to come to terms with your faith being their faith as well, then it will never be their faith. One of my daughters had to walk away from our faith, do some stupid things in relation to our faith, and has now come back to us. This happened over the course of about three years. It was heart-wrenching, and I spent a lot of sleepless hours in prayer. At all times she knew my stance on things, she knew that I was there for her and loved her, but she also knew that I wanted this to be an honest process. While I might want her to share my faith I also wanted her to discover for herself that it was what she needed rather than have me just tell her that. As I told her, "You may decide you hate white milk and only like chocolate. That's ok. Just don't pretend, for my sake, that you like the white milk. And don't toss all the milk out because we like different kinds." It was this open honesty in allowing her to explore her spirituality that allowed her to come back.

What does your church do to help these young people (or older lost-in-limbo ones) explore their identity? Do you help them to know they are a child of the King? Do you let people ask the hard questions, even the blasphemous ones, without getting all bent out of shape? Do you have a forum in the church or in your small groups where this is accepted, and maybe even expected? Do you have mentors for your young people other than their parents who can walk life with the young people on a regular basis, to be their sounding board and their example? Or do you have a church where people are expected to come and fit a mold of behavior and appearance? Even if we assume your mold is spot-on correct, they will stop coming. People in this age want to discover who they are, not be forced to be something they're not sure they want to buy into.

Relationship vs. Isolation

While relationships are important at every age and in every stage of development, relationships are of primary importance to young adults. It is in college that people often find their life partner, where they make close friendships that will often surpass those of their teenage years and last, like family, for a lifetime. The camaraderie formed in early jobs will also last forever. If these young adults don't go through this processes in a healthy way, they will, at best, become isolated individuals who feel unable to have relationships, or, at worst, be isolated by unhealthy relationships. And, if these same young adults come into your church and don't find the opportunity to make these same types of lasting, personal, committed relationships, they will isolate themselves from your church saying it is irrelevant to their lives.

What does your church do to help these young people (or older isolated ones) build healthy relationships? Do you have regular potlucks that are lengthy and relaxed? Do you have frequent social events that allow people to bond both in friendship and in the Lord? Is there time in your service for genuine joy, laughter, and the sharing of burdens in a non-formalized manner? Do people in your church hang out outside of church doing things friends would do, so that when they come to church, they are simply coming with their friends to another thing friends do; worship the Lord Jesus Christ? Or is church more of drudgery they have to endure with people they are not intimately connected to? If so, they will stop coming.

Practical Application

As with so many other things, we at B.A.C. began to meet these needs without thinking about Erick Erikson. Much of what we have done has arisen out of our small group beginnings, and from a desire of the founding families to keep a family atmosphere. I have noticed that unlike in other churches I have been a part of, when I have a good day and want to tell someone, I call my friends from church. When I have a bad day and need support, I call my friends from church. When I want to be silly and have fun, I call my friends from church. This comes because I learned to trust my church family, I learned they were safe people to be around in terms of autonomy and initiative (they're always letting me try new things!), and as a young adult, they were with me as I learned my identity and made my early relationships.

We were able to pass this on to others who have come in. I have never seen a church group so friendly that if someone comes in, they are immediately brought into a circle of potential friends who will be there for them. We have one lady who comes to church that is not a member on the books (though she is more faithful than most members!) who told me after her third visit that she loves how safe it is. In her old church if she asked a question she was treated in a way that made her feel judged. She said that at B.A.C. she had learned (by the third visit, no less) that she could ask anything, and disagree with anything, and we would still respect, accept, and love her. She has been one of our most faithful attendees.

About a year ago this lady came to me during potluck and said, "I have a question. I don't believe in Jesus' divinity." We sat there, in the middle of lunch, surrounded by all, and discussed this very openly. Others came and joined. She didn't feel ashamed or embarrassed; she felt no need to go somewhere private. Why? Because we are all friends and family and she felt safe to have that conversation in the presence of anyone who happened to be there. When was the last time you experienced that at church?

There are some practical things we do that allow people to worship in their current stage of development. The church loves children, and if they're loud, it's ok. Kids love to make noise, and the members love to hear the life that noise represents. There is a mother's room, but that is for those that desire it, not as a requirement. If anyone shows interest in doing anything, it is supported. Do you want to help the deacon with the roving microphone? Go for it! Do you have an idea for a new ministry? Explore it and tell us how we can help (no matter how young you are).

One of the things that I think is great is that our church is set up with a balcony that wraps around our worship area. The kitchen and dining area is up there. During the church, all the young people who are in adolescence (who, remember, are trying to figure out how to be industrious) will go up there and help prepare the food and dining area. You would think they are not getting anything out of the service, but they are routinely leaning over to listen to the speaker and interacting more than some of the adults (remember, we have an interactive service). Also, many of the items in Appendix D are things we have done at this church to build friendship among members.

Part 2

Connection Happens in Three Areas

This is a fact that I first learned in dealing with youth ministries, but it is true of all effective ministries. When people's lives are connected to the church, it is because they have found connection in three key areas: Friendship, Outreach, and Spiritual Growth. Ignore any combination of these, and your ministry will be less successful because some people will feel disconnected in some way.

Fellowship (Controlled Hang Time)

I knew the truth. Christians just didn't know how to have fun. Let's face it, in media that is how we are portrayed. The Christians are always trying to keep everyone from having fun, because, it seems, God is not interested in fun. Forget that He created the emotion of joy and the ability to laugh. Christians just don't have fun. And, before I was a Christian that is exactly what I thought.

And then I met Pastor Chris.

I had a friend who tricked me into going to his youth meetings. Yes, tricked. He said we would have fun at the local YMCA (which, to his credit, we did), but he never once told me that it was a Christian youth event. He probably knew that if he had, I would not have gone. At the door, I met Pastor Chris. He was big, with muscles big enough to intimidate Rambo. I quickly learned that this group loved to have fun, to make friends and that Pastor Chris was a big part of that.

I remember one time we were in the basement of their church making cookies for elderly shut-ins. I happened to glance at Pastor Chris just in time to see an impish look come over his face. The next thing I knew he was using those massive muscles to lift one of the other kids up in one arm, dump a bag of flour out on the table with his free hand, and then lay that kid down on in the flour and spin him like a top. Pastor Chris new how to have fun. Pastor Chris knew how to make friends. More importantly, I believe Pastor Chris knew enough to set the tone of fun and friendship and then get out of the way so others could have fun and make friends too.

It's not only young people who want to have fun and be with friends. When I was growing up, my parents got together with another couple every Sunday to share a meal and play card games. I have young adult friends who love to get together and play board games. When I visit elderly people in nursing homes, they often tell me about those that they "hang with" at the home, or bemoan how people don't come to see them. God made us social creatures, and we like to have friends and have fun with our friends. This is why I call fellowship "controlled hang time." If done right fellowship is really about friendship, and we "hang" with our friends. If it is a youth ministry, you want to control the hang time to some degree. Teenagers have a way of breaking things, and I'm sure you want your house back in one piece if at all possible.

Unfortunately, in many places, the church has become a place that people come to have an isolated experience of worship in a room full of people who are near strangers. Think I'm wrong? I was recently having a conversation with a church leader who is the president of a conference of over seventy churches. We were discussing the growth of B.A.C., and he was talking about the innovative worship style and how he wished more churches would catch that vision.

"You know," I said, "there is more to the growth of this church than just the worship style."

"Like what?"

"Well, when I'm happy and want to have fun, who do I call? My friends from B.A.C. When I'm having a horrible day, and I need to talk, who do I call? My friends from B.A.C. When I'm in great need, who do I call? My friends from B.A.C. When I just want to go out and be with my friends, who do I call? My friends from B.A.C."

And that is one of the keys to their success. This church, more than any other church I know, has learned how to be friends and family to anyone that walks in the door. As mentioned in a previous chapter, some of this is because of our background, some of it is because of our mission, and some of this is because of our intentional philosophy in sermons structure. But much of it is in the fact that we do things together to build friendships.

Around Thanksgiving time we turkey bowl. I mean we literally take frozen turkeys and bowl them at two-liter bottles of soda. There is nothing like seeing a soda bottle explode on impact from a frozen turkey, especially when the soda drenches the spouse of the bowler (this actually happened at another church where I introduced the idea of turkey bowling). That man got a trophy.

Once a year we have a mini-golfing tournament, complete with a trophy made by one of our members.

We have cooking challenges where teams have to make a themed meal using only the basic ingredients we provide (oil, salt, and other simple ingredients), and with what they can buy with the $20 we provide (they must provide receipts to prove their purchases were under $20). I never partook of these since I cannot cook. Then one of the members came up with an idea: a cooking challenge for the cooking challenged. I still lost!

Once, with some kids, we did a rock-a-thon. They had sponsors come forward and agree to pay a child a certain amount of money for every hour they rocked in a chair. The money was being raised to help one of our young people go on a mission trip. We borrowed about thirty rocking chairs and rocked away from 7:00 PM to 7:00 AM. The kids had access to food and pre-approved video games and pre-approved movies. If they had to get up or take a break for any reason, they simply signed out. What memories we have from that night.

Some people worry that by doing these types of activities, we will somehow lose site of our mission as a church. That is true if this is all we do. Remember, there are many more chapters in this book, next two are specifically vital to having a balanced church that has a mission to win souls. But being able to make and retain friends is a vital aspect of a healthy, well-balanced, growing church. Many of us have heard statistics such as:

- A person who enters a church and makes 0-3 friends has an almost 100% statistical probability of leaving and never returning.
- A person who enters a church and makes 4-5 friends has an almost 80% statistical probability of leaving and never returning.
- A person who enters a church and makes 6-8 friends has an almost 80% statistical probability of becoming a permanent member.
- A person who enters a church and makes 6-8 friends has an almost 100% statistical probability of becoming a permanent member.

(These figures are estimates based on several studies I have seen. They all give slightly different numbers, so I use the range above for each category rather than a specific number).

So, to those who question if it is proper for a church to have and emphasis on friendship, I have two questions for you: Would you prefer to be a friendly church that retains visitors, so you have a chance to present the gospel? Or would you rather be preaching to people who may not want to come back for lack of fellowship? In your church the choice is yours. In my church, we have decided to be a healthy church that includes fellowship. We don't neglect our theology or our mission. Unlike most churches, I go to we make sure that in the bulletin, on the screen, and in the sermon, our distinct message is preached. But we preach to people we hope to be friends with, and we are growing as a result.

Practical Application

Since this chapter has already been about what we do at B.A.C., let me use another church's experience for this section. An acquaintance of mine is currently pastoring a church in the Midwest. He's been there for only a few years, but his church is growing so fast that he is beginning to be recognized as an authority on church growth. His secret? Authentic friendship.

Each member of his church is encouraged to be part of a group of people that all enjoy a hobby. There are only two rules:
1. Join a group that does something you like.
2. Be an authentic Christian.

What types of groups are there that they join? There are basketball groups, groups that like to cook, groups that like to go to restaurants, groups that enjoy Bible studies, groups that like to sew, groups that like to get their little ones together to hang out, groups that like to build and fly drones, and so much more. Christians are in these groups. Non-Christians are in these groups. No matter if the other people are Christian or not, the members of this church don't check their Christianity at the door. They pray before they eat, the pray for safety in their sports, and they take a genuine interest in each other's lives. Eventually, someone feels safe enough to share something they are going through, and their group, made up people they trust because they have become friends, will pray for them and try to support them as only friends can do. And eventually, these people come to church to worship the God they have come to know because of their new friends.

How simple, and yet how powerful it is to simply be able to make friends and introduce them to Jesus through your regular behavior. No wonder friendship, fellowship, controlled hang time, or whatever you want to call it, is part of a healthy and growing church.

Service
(Not Just Physical)

Young people want to change the world, and social media companies latch onto this idea to drive their product. It is easy these days for a young person to feel that they can use their voice to make a difference. From the privacy of their bedroom, they can make videos, create memes for gifs, compose music, produce short films, and then post it on forums where literally millions of people can see it. Whether millions of people actually see their posts is irrelevant, they at least got their message "out there," and maybe, just maybe, it will have an impact.

And then they come to church and are expected to sit, have their voices silenced and be talked to about something that (from their perspective) may not connect with anything they are dealing with in the "real world," while in that very same "real world" things are happening and they can't do anything about it. My friends, there is a reason why these young people would often rather stay in their room with their phone rather than go to church, and it isn't always about entertainment.

Young people aren't the only ones that want to make an impact. For years we have talked about middle age crisis. Around forty years of age people begin thinking about career and life changes. We often joke that this is because they want to recapture their youth. And, while there may be some truth to that, I think those of us in that age group (and, by the way, I heard on a recent news report that the age for people to have a mid-life crisis is now averaging at 35) are realizing that what we've been doing is not rocking the world the way we wanted to rock it 20 years ago. You see, we all have desires to make some kind of difference. And our churches often are not providing ways for people to make the difference they feel they should, and so they go elsewhere to try and fill this need.

Over the past several decades the term "social justice" has become a hot-button word in some churches. Some believe it is the church's responsibility to be partakers in social justice movements, and others believe it is our duty to avoid them so we can focus on our God-given message. I am not getting into this fray, so please resist the temptation to equate this chapter with social justice. This chapter is dealing with a much more organic need that I believe God placed inside those that are filled with His Spirit: The need to make a difference for good in a world that is often controlled by evil. The Bible is filled with examples of this:

- Dorcas made clothes for the needy.
- The early church gave food, money, and lodging to those that were in need.
- In the first letter to Timothy, we are told we need to take care of our family members and widows.
- The Old Testament (yes, the Old Testament!) is filled with regulations making sure that the poor and lame can have food and aren't taken advantage of.
- How many people did Jesus heal and care for?

This is such a fundamental part of our human makeup, and is so clearly delineated in Scripture (the examples above are just a few of the many I could have cited) that when a church neglects this type of ministry people often, and naturally, feel a disconnect between them and their church, between their church and their community, and even between their church and God that they may stop coming.

Our denomination has something called Camp Meeting, where for about ten days people come from all over their region and worship and have fellowship. There are, of course, plenty of youth activities available to keep young people busy. For several years I was leading out in the early-elementary age group and noticed that the tent (yes, we use tents!) designated for the teens had low attendance. The faithful few were in the tent (often looking bored), many would be outside the tent just hanging out with friends, and even more, would not even make it to the tent.

One year I was asked to take over the teen tent, which I did. I made some immediate changes, one of which was doing daily service projects in the community. I told the kids that, as a long-time resident of that village, I knew there were many that did not like our Camp Meeting. They felt we all came and took from the community, but never gave back. I told them they could make a real difference if we spent two hours every morning during those ten days doing something practical for the community. We picked up garbage, cleaned the park and the beach, we painted picnic tables and garbage cans, we swept sidewalks, we painted trim on a house. Yes, the community appreciated all of this, and it went a long way towards building a better relationship with the community, but something else blew me away. Around eighty kids were showing up for community service every morning, but when we did something fun in the afternoon (like go roller skating or hiking) only about forty kids came.

Did you catch that? Twice as many young people came for community service than for fun. When I asked them why they said it was because they could hang out with their friends anywhere, but the service was providing them with a way to make an impact that they didn't get to do on their own. You see, people really do want to rock their world!

Practical Application

You say you don't have the money or resources to take on a service project, or that you don't have people physically able to do a manual labor project? That's ok! There are other ways to serve that aren't as intense. Let me share just two with you.

Most areas have local chapters of various civic organizations, and many of these organizations already have service projects going. You can simply partner up with one of these. I am a member of our local Lion's Club, which raises money every year to give scholarships to people as well as to get glasses and hearing aids for those that can't afford to get these items themselves. Every year they host a pancake breakfast on Super Bowl Sunday, the proceeds of which go to one of these great causes. I bring young people from the church to wait tables at this breakfast. There is no preparation, no funding required, no cleanup afterward (unless we volunteer it). We simply show up, bring food to people, and leave knowing that we helped someone see or hear better as a result.

Another service project that is not labor intensive is Make You Smile Ministry (MYSM). I had students in my school that wanted to do an evangelistic series. The fact that they wanted to do this was awesome, and I didn't want to tell them "no," but I did see one problem. "Who is going to come?" I asked them. Did they or their parents know anyone in the community? This may seem like a strange question, but they were primarily children of faculty at a religious boarding school, which is a very self-contained community. All of their contacts were already church members. We decided to pray about how we could introduce ourselves to the community (who just thought we were a strange community "up on the hill"), and make friends that may one day come to an evangelistic event.

One day my father sent me a YouTube link to an organization called "Improve Everywhere." I loved what this organization was doing to create shared experiences and memories for people in New York City.

In fact, I didn't just love it; I was inspired by it. I showed the link to my students and asked them if they thought we could do something similar in our little village with the intent of making people smile while introducing ourselves to the community. They already think we're weird, so let's be weird for fun!

Thus MYSM was born. Once every month we would go out into the community to do something that would make people smile. We walked invisible dogs. We did air band marching parades. We gave out hi-fives. We had a blast, and we kept track of how many people we made smile. During our air band marching parade (the last event I did before leaving that school) we had one person honk their horn at us, turn around, go to the local store, and drive by us again and throw candy at us. The businesses on the sidewalk came to know us by this point and came out bringing us water. We made friends and connections, and we made people smile. In this world, that is a great service.

When we went out for MYSM, we also brought invitations to our church's family game night. On a few occasions, there were more people from the community at our game nights than there were church members. They enjoyed the table games, the gym activities, and the weird events we did (we just kept capitalizing on that "weird" thing!), such as bowling frozen turkeys at two-liter bottles of soda.

The point is this; when you think of service, it doesn't have to be manual labor. It needs to make a difference, it needs to have an element of fun in it, and it has to be something that will be appreciated by both those who give and receive the service.

Meaningful, Rigorous Bible Study

Let me be honest, as a teacher, if I taught my subject areas the way we normally give Bible studies I would be fired.
Imagine being a fourth grader working on dividing fractions. You teacher shows you one time, and one time only, how to multiply the first fraction by the reciprocal of the second fraction and reduce, and calls this multiplication division with no real explanation as to why. He/she may even show you how to simply before multiplying (I mean dividing?). But they show you once and only once. You are told there is a book if you can't remember exactly how it works. Oh, and by the way, there is never any review on this topic, or any other topic, ever.
If I taught your fourth-grade child math this way, you would probably ask for a parent/teacher conference to let me know (hopefully very politely) how badly I was hurting your child's academic future. And you would have every right!

There are many reasons why teaching this way is so bad. It doesn't use multiple intelligences (see the first chapter to review that one), so I am leaving out 8/9 of the strengths that children might have, so I am not connecting with them. I am not taking into account that, developmentally, children need much review (and for fractions, I bet many of you adults do too!). And, in no way, am I entering into the life of the child and connecting with them with this teaching method. Jesus did that. It is called discipleship, and it should not be surprising that a student will try harder and succeed to greater lengths when they are working with someone they are connected to in a positive way.
For these reasons and more, teaching math, or social studies, or language, or any other topic this way is bad teaching. I would have been fired for that. Currently, as an administrator, if I have a teacher who is doing this I will try to mentor and help them, but if they don't improve, I will need to fire them and replace them. It is simply not good teaching.

But this is exactly how many of us teach the Bible.

Think about it. How did you learn Bible truths? I know many people in many denominations who, sometimes guided by an experienced person and sometimes not, are given lesson sheets. Read it, look up the verses, fill in the blanks, and move on. No review ever. Rarely is there a connection to anything practical in one's life. And this only uses 1/9, maybe 2/9 of the multiple intelligences. And then we as church leaders wonder why these truths are not sinking into the heads and hearts of our people and not making an impact. We are Christians doing ministry for the Lord Jesus Christ. We must find a better way of teaching the Bible in our Bible studies.

As mentioned several other times in this book, I am taking for granted that you are praying for the infilling and guidance of the Holy Spirit when you prepare and execute and follow up on your Bible studies. If not, you need to begin doing so. No method I give will be effective for eternity without the Lord's blessing, so begin there if you haven't done so already. After that, you can look at what comes next.
Appendix F provides a model for interactive Bible study. This is just that, a model. It can be torn apart, discarded, remolded, and used or not used in many different ways. It is not intended to be used as the way to study the Bible, but to give you a starting point from which you can build your own method and style of study. But, before you can really look at that, let me tell you about closet learning.

The human brain is like a closet, and the information you store there is like the clothing all ready to go on hangers. Before you can hang up your clothing, you need one very important item: the bar. If you don't have the bar, then you are doing nothing more than throwing the clothing into the closet where it piles up on the floor. Later when you want to get your clothing, if you can find what you're looking for, it is wrinkled and nasty, and you probably won't even want to wear it. It is much better to hang the bar up first so the clothing can be placed on the bar in an organized manner the preserves the original intent of the item hanging there.

The model that is presented in Appendix F is designed to help as many people as possible get a bar placed in their brain. It will not go in depth in any one doctrinal point, but it will set the stage to where multiple doctrinal points – such as the divinity and humanity of Christ, the Trinity, the intimacy of Jesus with His people, the state of the dead, the resurrection, God's omniscience, and many more – can be revisited later at a much deeper level. But in this lesson, the connections are made in a way that a bar can be put in the mind of many different types of people.

Since this is a model for an interactive Bible study, let's talk for a moment about what it means to be interactive. Being interactive is more than simply posing questions or engaging in conversation so that you are not the only one talking. Being interactive means that the brain inside of every person participating is doing just that; it's participating. In an interactive Bible study, every effort is made by the facilitator to engage people, so they are taking an active role in their learning, even if they are being silent in the process. You want them to be processing the information, connecting it to their lives. For very few people this will happen in a stand-and-deliver classroom. It is much more affective if a facilitator thinks about all the things we've already talked about in this book, particularly in the first two chapters. To that end, this model lesson uses interpersonal, intrapersonal, spiritual, bodily-kinesthetic, visual-spatial, and linguistic intelligences in dealing with topics that are relevant to the developmental stages of different ages of people.

Let's be honest. This is time-consuming. It is much easier to pick up a premade publication or lesson to which you can stand up and talk or try to lead a discussion. Many class facilitators can do that with very little prep time and anxiety. This, on the other hand, takes much more short-term prep time for the one lesson, but it also takes quite a bit of long-term planning. If you started out with this model lesson, you need to be thinking about which topic(s) you will cover in the coming weeks and months and be planning at least an outline of where you want to go. This is a much more intense manner of teaching, but that is why it is so affective. If you are not sure if it is affective, give it a try for one lesson. Give it the proper planning and practice first so that it can go smoothly, but do one lesson and see if there is a difference that you want to continue. If there are elements that don't work for you (some churches may find the video "too much" for their church culture, for example), then tweak it to work for you. Just try it, and see if there are more connections that result from it than from your regular Bible study.

Practical Application

This chapter and its appendix by nature are just practical. There is not a lot to add other than to tell you of some success with this very model lesson. As I write these words, I am coming off a series of training that other church administrators and myself have been doing across Upstate New York. At eight events we have presented training members of about seventy churches. At many of these events, we have young people who are burned out on Bible study and church. We have older people who are skeptical that young people even want to study the Bible (they do!) and that seems to be burned out on Bible study themselves. By about halfway through the model lesson, there are lots of smiles by all parties, laughter, and, most importantly, connections between the participants (of all ages) and the Scripture. Sometimes I even have to remind them that we are not really doing the lesson but exploring the method of how to give a lesson and make them stop discussing the topic. That's when I know that they are hooked and ready to keep getting into the Bible.

Part 3

Connection Happens More Than One Day A Week

Feeling overwhelmed yet? You should! There is a lot that goes into a ministry of connection. It is more than you can possibly fit into one day a week like we often try to do in our churches. In fact, it is more than can go into two or three days a week. A system must be developed to make the church family be connected throughout the week. This will take organization, intentionality, and all hands on deck.

Ministry of Presence

Let's talk about youth and young adult ministries for a moment. Pastor Dale was an amazing man. This humble pastor was instrumental in helping me commit my life to Jesus, and his method was quite simple. I don't think he knew about connecting through multiple intelligences, and I don't think he knew about connecting through levels of development, and I'm sure he didn't know about using the three different areas of connection ministry. But he did know about being present.

- Pastor Dale came to my house, listened to me play guitar.
- Pastor Dale met my parents.
- Pastor Dale visited me at my college.
- Pastor Dale took my calls in the middle of the night.
- Pastor Dale came to my birthday party.
- Pastor Dale was present in my life.

Contrast this with disturbing stories and examples that I have witnessed and that young people have complained to me about on different occasions.

- Pastors come to the house to visit with adults, and maybe have a passing comment of the young people.
- Pastors shake the hands of adults and do small talk at the back of the sanctuary but say nothing to the young people passing right in front of them.
- Pastors who never reach out to the children in their schools (K-collegiate). If they're not in the church, they don't get any attention.
- Birthday parties? Pastors go to those?
- Pastors who are not present in their lives.

Let's broaden the scope from youth and young adult ministry to any ministry. An effective minister is present in the life of their congregants. Are you a primarily aging church? You need to be present in the life of your older members. Are you a church with a good mix of age groups? You need to be present in the lives of all age groups. In short, who is your church ministering to? Be present in their lives.

"Now wait a minute!" I can hear some of you saying. "Do you have any idea all the things I am responsible for? How can I be that present in so many lives?" Yes, I do have some knowledge of your many responsibilities. You have to have time to prepare your sermon. You have emergencies that you have to respond to. You have multiple boards and committees that you attend, and even chair, both for your local congregation and possibly for higher levels of your denomination. You have new ministries you are trying to promote, revive, or create. In short, you have to be the CEO, manager, and supervisor for a large corporation. And you need to find a way to have personal time and time with your family. So how, indeed, can you make time to minister directly to every member and be meaningfully present in their lives?

Simply, it can't all be done in one day every week, and you can't do it all alone. There are some things you can do, some of which have already been mentioned, that don't take much time at all.

- When you're shaking hands at the back of the sanctuary, make sure you go out of your way to get everyone.
- Don't commit yourself to teach a class every time your church gathers for worship. Leave time to visit other classes, and make sure you visit every classroom.
- When you visit a home, take time to connect with every person in that home.
- If you're visiting a school, take time to connect with students and staff alike.

These items require no real extra outlay of time, but just a switch in our emphasis and thinking. These simple changes alone can go a long way, but it is not enough. I advise that you work on building your ministry team so that many hands can make light work. Just keep in mind, building up a ministry team in order to get more done only helps you to get more done. Building up a ministry team in order to ensure more connections can be made by you and other leaders helps you to get more ministry done. It will be important to train your ministry team members with this idea that dividing the work helps more ministry get done.

See Appendix H for ideas on how to train your ministry team for connections.

Practical Applications

I have been a part of several churches that use different methods to organize their leadership. In one church the elders were divided between the ministries so that each ministry had a direct contact with the ministerial team, and the ministerial team met a few times a month to make sure everyone was in the loop. This is a good model for accountability and communication, but more is needed for connection. This should free the pastor up to make more visits instead of more administration. And the elder in charge should also be visiting with the people in their "department." And visiting means visiting, not meeting, not brainstorming, not evaluating, though all of that is appropriate. Sometimes you just need to visit to build connections.

I have been in churches where members (sometimes officers, sometimes not) are put on a schedule to the main adult class every weekend. This frees up the pastor to go to every classroom. They can sit and participate as a class member instead of being the leader. They can play with the kids, singing their songs and doing their crafts. They can go to the teen class and play devil's advocate to get the teacher frustrated and make the teens smile.

I have been to churches where a committee is designated to plan family-friendly church events. The pastor should be at these events and just play with the kids, sit with the guys trading stories, and doing whatever else a "regular guy" does at such things. Show support, but don't create, organize, and work the event. Have some type of ministry team do this. You can give advice, but delegate this so that you can use the time to connect.

Several good church leaders I have worked with keep the focus of connection ministry at the forefront of the conversation at every meeting. They are always presenting to their teams the question, "How will this help us connect with _____?" If you're not intentional, you will become an administrator instead of a pastor.

For smaller churches that don't have a lot of people, a ministry team may be unmanageable or impossible. In these situations, your church is the ministry team. Use your small numbers to create a family atmosphere in which connection is natural. As the group grows, be purposeful in how you maintain that atmosphere.

The key for this section is that, while there are many ways to organize a ministry team, you must, and I mean must be purposeful in maintaining a commitment to connection. Organization for organization's sake is not good enough. Organization to improve the quality and quantity of connections you can make as a leader to those you are ministering to is the goal.

Ministry of Recognition

Just last week I was at a meeting of administrators. Understand, I have been serving my church in my area for almost twenty years, and I've been engaged in leadership at one level or another for about twelve years. I have known all the pastors and teachers in our denomination in Upstate New York for the majority of that time, and have been in the upper level of our leadership for almost three years. As such, I also have a good working relationship with most of the leadership one the next tier up from us, which governs our denomination in all of New York, New England, and Bermuda.

It was at a meeting of Administrators from all over this region that it happened. We were discussing a matter of importance, and I asked the chair to be recognized for a comment. He said, "We will now here a comment from…." Nothing. Dead silence with an empty blank stare. I looked at him and knew at that moment that he had not only forgotten my name but that he really had no idea who I was. After a moment of uncomfortable silence, the leader next to him whispered my name (loud enough for all of us to hear) and the chair snapped back into gear and let me speak.

Please understand something, I have nothing against this fine leader. I didn't take it personally, and I didn't go sulking off to lick some imaginary wound. There is too much work for Jesus to be done for that! But shortly after the meeting another administrator came up to me and said, "I'm sorry. It must be hard being that low on the totem pole that he doesn't even know who you are."

Now, I don't know if this administrator's assessment of the situation was accurate, and I frankly don't care. However, it is interesting to note that even among adults it is common to feel that if someone doesn't know your name, then you are not important to them. This may or may not be true. I can't keep my daughter's names straight. Does that mean I don't care about them? Absolutely not! But, if after all these years of caring for them I honestly didn't know their names, then that would be a very different matter.

Do you know the names of every person you minister to? After all this time caring for them do you know their name? If you don't, it doesn't matter what your heart actually says, the message you are sending to them is that you don't care for them. And if adults get this message, it is received even more powerfully by young people.

Because I have a hard time keeping my children's (all girls) names straight, I began calling everyone in my family honey. They didn't seem to mind, so I started doing the same thing to my students. This was during my first teaching assignment, and I thought that the young people wouldn't mind. One day a bunch of my seventh-grade boys came to me and told me just how very much they really did mind! I expected that it was because the term "honey" was not tough enough for these young men, but then they and the girls began to inform me how much it hurt them that I didn't know their names. I heard their complaint loud and clear and began calling them by there names. This one change completely revolutionized our classroom atmosphere because now they felt cared for, respected, important, and connected to me.

Ever since that time I have taken time to memorize the names of those I am ministering to. If I am in a school our first day has plenty of icebreaker games designed to help me learn their names. If I'm at camp, I spend considerable time with each cabin learning their names and making fun of myself when I can't get it right. When I'm in a church, I freely admit I am bad at names and ask permission upfront to ask adults their names repeatedly until I get it right, giving them permission to pick on me and correct me as much as they want.

Usually, all these groups really appreciate my efforts, and natural connections result. I learn about those I am ministering to very quickly because they naturally trust a person who cares enough about them to purposefully learn their names. They tell me their joys and pains and about their hobbies and work. In short, there is a reason God says that He knows us by Name; that knowledge creates an immediate connection, and as His ambassadors, we need to do the same.

Practical Application
Work with your ministry team on devising ways for all of you to learn everyone's names. The bigger your church is, the more daunting this task is. But it is necessary. The moment your parishioners think you don't know their name is the same moment you may lose a connection and be unable to regain it. There are plenty of resources available to help you do this. There are books on icebreakers, team building, community building, and so forth.

One church I attended for a number of years had over three hundred members. I praised God when I learned that the church had a directory of names, phone numbers, and pictures. I studied that nightly for months until I had all the names right. If you don't have such a directory, then use postcards, take pictures yourself (with permission of course), or do anything else you can do to make a system for you and your ministry team to learn the names of everyone.

One last piece of advice on this topic. Learn the names of young people. Don't ignore their parents in this, but don't ignore the kids either. Many adults, if you only know the name of their kids but you don't know their name, may feel that you are some kind of weirdo. If you know their names but not their kid's names they may feel that you really don't care about them because you don't care enough about the most important people in their lives. But, if you know their names and the names of their kids, then they see you care about them and their family, and they will feel an instant connection to you that will aid your ministry in a significant way.

Ministry of Discipleship

"We don't want to be told what not to do. We want to be shown how to live." Take a wild guess who has stated these words to other leaders and me time and time again. If you said new believers you are dead wrong. The speakers of these words, at least to the leaders I work with and myself, are those being raised "in the church," or in other words, those being raised in Christian homes and who have had a Christian upbringing.

This comes as a surprise to many people. You would think that people "raised in the church" would be automatically connected to the church they were raised in, to the God they had modeled before them, and have a clear view of what it means to be a disciple of Jesus Christ. But the fact of the matter is, that is simply not the case.

Remember Erick Ericson's Theory of Human Development from part one? Remember what the big question teens are trying to deal with at their age? It's all about identity. It is during this phase (not in college, as many suggest) that either their parents' religion becomes their religion, or it doesn't. It is during this phase that their parents' God becomes their God, or He doesn't. And it is precisely this phase of seeking one's own identity that makes them distrustful of parents.

You may be the best parent in the world. Ana's parents were (not her real name). I had watched her grow from a young seven-year-old to a sixteen-year-old. Her parents were great people, great Christians, and friends of mine. He is a pastor and a youth director, so he has counseled and mentored countless young people. And yet, every one of their children sought out another adult during their teen years, and I was her chosen mentor. She would routinely come to me to ask questions that I knew for a fact she had discussed with her parents, but she needed to hear it from someone else. There were times when she came to me with problems that she did not want her parents to know about.

Once we were at a church camp, and she came to find me at a late hour in the night. We sat and talked in a public place (always be careful to avoid temptation and protect your reputation) until even later. As she poured out her cares to me, I happened to look outside and saw her father coming up the outside stairs towards us. He looked in, saw us talking, and walked away. Later he told me that he knew she needed to talk to someone and that she would not talk to him. This wise father knew she needed a mentor to guide her through her doubts, questions, and troubles, and he allowed her to have one. Today she is a happily married young Christian lady who is active in her church.

Do the young people who are raised in your church have access to those types of mentors? Others need mentoring too, and if you want more information on that, then you should turn to part five. But you cannot neglect those of every age who have been raised in the church. They may look good, but they have doubts and questions like everyone else. They feel judged by people who tell them what to do without having a close relationship first. And they feel judged by people who do have a close relationship with them tell them they're wrong but don't model and explain to them what is right and why. In short, they need someone safe who can be their guide as they walk life together.

Practical Application

You and your ministry team need to develop a training system for mentors and a mentoring program your church can use. Whatever your model it must have the following elements:

- It must include training on avoiding (as in not committing), identifying, and properly dealing with abuse.
- It must include some type of vetting and background check strategy. You can never be too careful with who you choose to work with kids or others needing mentoring.
- It must be flexible enough and broad enough to be conducted in church and during the week. Remember, ministry happens more than one day a week.
- It must be geared to the needs of your members.
- It must include ministry to "those raised in the church."
- It must be easy and common sense. If you develop a complicated system, it will not be attractive to mentors or mentees.

Do not relinquish participation/leadership in any area that requires mentorship, including youth clubs. You can share that responsibility, and I recommend that you do. Be willing to take a second, third, or fourth place leadership role. Maybe you only show up to a fraction of the events to lead out and have a part, but don't give up any of them entirely. All members, but especially youth, need to see their church leaders and pastors involved in the ministry that is reaching out to them. They must see you as a leader who cares and is connected!

Part 4

Connecting From The Pulpit

While much of a ministry of connection takes place outside the pulpit, there are some things that you can put into practice that will help you connect. This section will not help you improve your skills as a biblical scholar. It is intended to help you take the knowledge God has blessed you with and connect it into the hearts and minds of your listeners. It is taken for granted that you are praying for the Holy Spirit to be with you, so we will not cover that (if you are not praying for this then it imperative that you begin!). Instead, we look at how you as a public speaker can better connect with your audience. While it is true that preachers of the gospel, because they have a message far and above any other message given by any other speaker, should not be reduced to cheap tricks and fads, neither should they, because their message is far and above any other message given by any other speaker, be ignorant of public speaking skills that could improve their ability to connect to their audience.

Ideas To Help People Connect With Your Message

Please understand that every suggestion in this chapter is just that: a suggestion! Not one of them is a hard fast rule written in stone. Every one of these I use in my practice regularly, but I have also disregarded every one of these when the time is right. For example, I typically keep my stories short, so I don't have anyone wandering off. However, there are times when I feel the Spirit moving, and I have everyone in rapt attention, and so I keep going. Other times I have to shorten up my stories even more than I suggest. Whatever the suggestion is, consider it a tool for your preaching tool belt. Use it when you can, but feel free to use a different tool, even tools that are not in my tool belt, when it is necessary.

Get Out And Move!
In some cultures, the pulpit or the "desk" is considered sacred ground. You get behind that pulpit and don't you dare move. In other cultures it is considered more relaxing, and therefore appropriate, to get move around the stage. I am in favor of getting out and moving. Not just out from behind the pulpit, but out from behind your comfort zone. I like to move up and down the isles, using that time to show my visual aid, touch people (appropriately of course), and have what looks like intimate conversations with members of the congregation. Depending on the size of your congregation this may not be possible. But when you can pull it off this really helps connect with your listeners.

Be Human, Be Personal, Be You, Be Direct
Tell stories. People love stories. Tell stories about you. People love it when you become human and show your weaknesses. While there are times you've done good things, make sure you share your failures as well. Don't always be the hero; that makes you too distant. Be human. Be personal. Be you, in all your strengths and weaknesses; in all your glories and failures. And be direct. If the story about you (or the story about anything) takes twenty minutes, then you most likely lost some of your listeners along the way.

It's About Time

Not only your stories, but your sermons as a whole should be short and sweet. Sometimes we are afraid if we don't go long and show all the learning we have regarding particular words or languages or passages then we will be robbing the people of their meat, and they will go away hungry. But I ask you, is your knowledge about words and languages and the rest the meat or is it the garnish? You definitely want your people to get the meat, but you don't want them choking on basil leaves before the meat ever gets to them. If your extras are dragging your sermon out, then cut them from the sermon. Again, be direct and make sure they get the meat.

I used to be an elder that preached regularly at my church of about three hundred members. The pastor who preached there regularly preached what I considered fantastic sermons. I was spiritually fed. But his sermons were usually 35-40 minutes. That didn't bother me, but it bothered my children. They would try really hard to pay attention sometimes, and they even had worksheets for them to color or fill in that had to do with the sermon. But they were just lost most of the time. In contrast, when I preached I tended to construct my sermons with the kids in mind. They were short sermons, only 15-20 minutes in length. I got to the point quickly and used strategies to make my point memorable. I figured that adults wouldn't mind. They knew I was a teacher after all and would forgive me. Besides, they got to eat lunch early!

I was surprised when older members of the congregation, even some of the "old pillars of the church" began coming to me and thanking me for my sermons and letting me know they were looking forward to my next one. Yes, they liked getting out early for lunch, but they also enjoyed getting their spiritual food garnish-free. They didn't dislike the pastor and his sermons; they just connected with less effort to the shorter sermons that got straight to the point.

Since that time I have experimented with how short is too short, and what garnishes I can get away from (sometimes a little Greek, Hebrew, or word study is important). I have learned that 20-25 minutes seems to be the optimum length for congregations, and I give the near the beginning after my attention-getter, but only if it can be used to really add flavor to the meat.

Two Way Street

I grew up as the second youngest of six. When you try to speak at that rank in the family, you are not always able to complete your thought without someone putting their two cents in. I am in a profession where everyone gets paid to talk, so when I get to talk with others in my profession, I don't always get to complete my thought without someone putting their two cents in. I live with five other people in my house, all females. I don't want to be guilty of perpetuating any stereotypes, but in my house, it is difficult to get your thoughts out without someone else putting their two cents in.

Is it any wonder that when I first started preaching, I liked the idea that I could finally get my point across without interruption? The entirety of my thought process could finally be laid out for everyone to see and hear and I could take the time I needed to in order to make that a reality. I think we all as preachers like this to one degree or another. The problem is that being able to lay one's own thoughts out does not guarantee that others are making connections with God, the Bible, the church, or with other members. For this reason, I have begun using interactive sermons (see the model sermon below for more on this).

Like interactive Bible studies, interactive sermons are more than just letting people interrupt you to talk and share their ideas (though this happens and you need to get used to it), but it is the process of structuring your sermons so that people are challenged to really wrestle with the information and apply it to their lives. I use multiple intelligences, Erikson's Theory of Human Development, challenges to people with how they can use the information immediately to make a difference in some way, and the other suggestions in this chapter to try and encourage them to interact, not with me, but with the message of the day, with the Bible, and with the God of the Bible.

Proper Presentation Software Usage

I know I said there are no hard-and-fast rules, but if any of these should be it would be this one. I have heard many church leaders say that if you just put the information on a PowerPoint, then you will keep kids attention. Wrong! Just ask any teacher who put their lecture on a PowerPoint if that kept them all awake. Every teacher knows that it just doesn't work that way.

Repeatedly I have seen presenters (pastors, teachers, and others) take the words that they are saying and put them, verbatim, on slides. It's like reading your paper to the class with it also up on the screen for them to read. The effect is to put them to sleep, not to aid in connection. This is now how to use presentation software.

    Instead, use presentation software to do what you can't do otherwise. Want to show the layers of the Grand Canyon as you are discussing evolution and creationism, but you can't afford to take your whole church there? Want to show the wonders of God as seen in the heavens but can't have church service at night at an observatory? Want to show how the armor of God in Ephesians relates to our lives today but forgot your breastplate at home? Or, on a more serious note, you want to highlight particular words in a passage of Scripture and connect them to similar words in other passages of Scripture? All of these are examples of times when presentation software can enhance your sermon by allowing you to show or do something that you couldn't show or do without it. That is presentation software at it's best. Avoid using it at its worst; don't just show a slide that says what you are saying.

Practical Application

    To give you an idea of how to put this all together I have included a model sermon format in Appendix H. I have used this type of format many, many times with young children, with teens, with young adults, and with the older saints. It is effective with all age groups. But know your congregation. If something about this format would be troubling to them or preventing them from getting the meat of the message, then alter it. Throw it out if you have to. But feel free to experiment with it to see if it will help foster connections between your members, God, and the Bible.

Part 5

Pulling It All Together

The point of having a ministry of connections is to use those connections to make disciples for Jesus Christ. This is part of the church's Great Commission. Discipleship is all about connections…at least when it is done the way Jesus did it.

Discipleship Jesus' Way

I don't know about you, but for the longest time when I thought about the part of the Great Commission that says we need to make disciples, I found that completely overwhelming. I mean, what does that even mean? What helped me was when I learned the difference between discipleship Jesus' way and discipleship as it had been done before Jesus.

In Israel, during the time of Jesus, there was a clear-cut path for anyone who wanted to be a disciple. First young Jewish boys (girls could not be disciples in that culture) around the age of five or six would begin going to their version of elementary school called Bet Sefer. The emphasis for this school was memorizing the Torah, what we call the Old Testament. A young boy did not memorize at least two Books of the Law by age twelve or thirteen and was not able to answer questions on those selections would be considered a failure. They were done, cast aside, unworthy to pursue discipleship and a master. They must go and learn a trade.

Those that succeeded at this level would then go to their version of high school, called Bet Midrash. If you're at all familiar with Jesus' clashes with the Pharisees and the teachers of the law, then you know that it was often over their traditions, which was called the Oral Torah. It was during their "high school" years at Bet Midrash that young men focused on the Oral Torah. The written Torah was still studied and memorized, but the emphasis was on how it related to the oral tradition and to one's life, and the young men were expected to show strict rigidity to these traditions. If you succeed, you have proven yourself worthy to find a master rabbi. If not, learn a trade.

Those that did find a master rabbi had to go and convince that rabbi that they were worthy to be a disciple. They would be tested on their memorization, their knowledge of both Oral and Written Torah, and they were scrutinized to see if they were strict in their keeping of tradition. If they were met with approval, then they were considered a Talmid, or disciple.

Just thinking about this type of life leaves me exhausted and a bit frustrated. I know that if I were living back, then I probably would have flunked out at the Bet Sefer stage and been learning a trade at about seven years of age. That was the fate of most young boys. That was most certainly the fate of Peter, James, John, Matthew, and the other disciples. Remember, Jesus found them at their trade. They were fishing, collecting taxes, and so forth. They had flunked out of school and had been deemed unworthy to be someone's disciples. But Jesus chose them anyway, and walked life with them to show them what God is like. That is what it means to make disciples.

There is no trick or how-to manual when it comes to making disciples. There is only the Jesus method. Come alongside others and do life with them, doing your best to show what Jesus is like in the process. You don't have to live homeless with them for three years as Jesus did. You don't need to wander the countryside for three years as Jesus did. You don't need to bless them with miraculous abilities like Jesus did (good thing too!). These were all a part of preparing them for apostolic ministry. There were many disciples that followed Jesus that didn't do any of these things with Jesus, at least not on a regular basis. They were not being called to apostolic ministry either. They were disciples. They were people who accepted Jesus' invitation to do life together, and they followed Him.

As you work with people – young people, old people, middle-aged people – if you are going to be effective in fulfilling the Great Commission you will need to do life with them. They will need to become like family to you. That can be uncomfortable, especially because Jesus came to help the sick, not the healthy. But comfort has nothing to do with it; discipleship has everything to do with it. Get ready to know their joys and their pains, their heartaches and their triumphs, their sicknesses, and their quirks. Get ready to spend time at their house, at their school, with their family. This is why Part 3 of this book is so important; that is where the discipleship begins. Where it ends depends on how well they learn of Jesus in the process, and how well you transmit the vision of how a Christian lives as Christ's ambassadors on earth.

Practical Application

Prayer, prayer, prayer. You can follow every last word in this book, but if you are not praying for Jesus to live in and through you, then you will not make any disciples for Him. Only as you let Jesus work through you will those you are doing life with see Him, be drawn to Him, and become disciples too. For that is the point; not to make disciples for you, but to make disciples for Him. So pray; pray hard, pray long, and pray for specific individuals.

Claim promises. You will never be perfect. Those you do life with, if you are truly doing life with them and not putting on a charade, will see you fail and fall. That's ok. Let them see you get back up claiming the promises of Scripture. Claim God's forgiveness. Claim God's grace. Claim God's remaking you into a new creature. Always, always point to God and His Word, and claim His promises openly and often.

Don't be afraid. God will go with you, even until the end of the age.

Appendices

Appendix A

Suggestions For Using Multiple Intelligences In Your Ministry For Connecting Individuals To Your Teachings

Below is a list of ideas for using Multiple Intelligence in your ministry. Don't just think about this for your sermon and church service. These are ideas that can be used elsewhere, such as during youth group meetings or outreach activities. This is not an inclusive list, and you will notice there is some overlap. Try to see how you can use these ideas to connect people to learning about God.

Spatial Intelligence	• Use presentation software to illustrate something that your words alone cannot. Make the slides visually appealing and meaningful, not just a verbatim resuscitation of what you are saying. • Use physical, concrete objects in your sermons or activities.
Musical Intelligence	• Make sure the music, no matter what style, is well rehearsed with your best musicians, and that the songs are chosen to help highlight the theme of the day's message.
Interpersonal Intelligence	• Use interactive sermons with discussion questions built in throughout the sermon, not just at the end.

	- Develop a culture where it is appropriate for the congregation to interrupt the speaker to add insight or ask questions.
- Have relaxed, prolonged (as in lengthy) fellowship meals. Yes, that will mean you are sacrificing part of your afternoon. But if you're connected, then you're with the people you want to be with anyways.
- Do some research into what educators call cooperative learning techniques. One of my favorites is called Think-Pair-Share. Here is how it works. Instead of simply asking a question, to which the same few individuals will always provide answers, ask the question and ask the group to think to themselves about it for a bit (intrapersonal intelligence). Then ask them to share what they think with someone next to them (interpersonal intelligence). Then they can share with the group.
Intrapersonal Intelligence	- Do some research into what educators call cooperative learning techniques. One of my favorites is called Think-Pair-Share. Here is how it works. Instead of simply asking a question, to which the same few individuals will always provide answers, ask the question and ask the group to think to themselves about it for a bit (intrapersonal intelligence).

	Then ask them to share what they think with someone next to them (interpersonal intelligence). Then they can share with the group. • Don't just focus on the theoretical or abstract nature of theology, but find practical applications to everyday life. • Provide time for journaling and deep reflection.
Bodily-Kinesthetic Intelligence	• Find a way to build meaningful movement into your ministry. This could be through hand motions, standing or raising of hands in response to questions, using icebreakers, or providing a meaningful project for them to work on. • In your small groups use icebreakers that require physical movement and teamwork. • Provide time for journaling and deep reflection.
Naturalist Intelligence	• Do things outside, or bring nature items as learning objects. • Explore the various nature parables Jesus told, and bring nature items to help illustrate them. • Use presentation software or other media to show nature scenes, items, or sounds that you can't bring into your ministry easily.

Linguistic Intelligence	• Use word study in your sermon preparation and presentation. • Discuss the literary elements found in the passage you are studying. • Do a book club ministry. • Study a particular book of the Bible and bring in many other literary resources. • Learn, no, perfect the art of storytelling.
Mathematical/Logical Intelligence	• Focus on the number patterns in the Bible. • Look at the prophecies that revolve around numbers. • Study the logic of how truths/doctrines fit together. • Use apologetics.
Spiritual Intelligence	• All of the above. • See the next chapter. • See Appendix B.

Appendix B

Suggestions For Using Spiritual Intelligences For Connecting With God

Below are some suggestions by layer. This is not an inclusive list, with some items overlapping. Feel free to disagree with my placement, but please feel free also to experiment.

Love The Lord With All Your Heart
- Give hugs.
- Gift/card giving ministries.
- Have great greeters at the door.
- Potluck ministries.
- Clown ministries.
- Divorce recovery/prevention ministries.
- Abuse recovery ministries.

Love The Lord With All Your Soul
- Prayer ministry.
- Divorce recovery/prevention ministries.
- Abuse recovery ministries.
- Mentorship/discipleship ministries.

Love The Lord With All Your Mind
- Small group Bible studies.
- Book clubs.
- Join/create think tanks to support a need. Those that love with their strength can carry out your plans.
- Make long range and short range ministry plans for the church.
- Develop a mission statement.

Love The Lord With All Your Strength
- Service activities (see Appendix E for examples).
- Get involved with a worthy charitable cause.
- Adopt a need, such as a grandparent in a nursing home, or raise

funds to plant a church or sponsor a mission trip.
- Speaking of mission trips…
- Begin a social media ministry.
- Feed the homeless.
- Clown ministries.
- Potluck ministries.

Appendix C

Suggestion For Using Erikson's Theory of Human Development To Create Connections Between The Church And The Members

Trust vs. Mistrust
- Scrap the idea of a mother's room as a necessity. It is an option. When parents feel that their kid needs to go to a quiet place they will go there. They don't need to feel that their kids are being relegated to a back corner just because they are a kid. Their children will pick up on this and will learn not to trust the church.
- Work purposefully and hard to create an environment where loud, messy children are accepted with joy for the simple joy of having the children there.
- Offer parenting classes so parents can learn how to best fill the needs of their children.
- In your classes use curriculum that purposefully teaches them that God is there for them, loves them, and wants to care for them.

Autonomy vs. Shame
- Let children shadow any of the officers.
- Give children meaningful work at the church work bees.
- Let the children help pick up the offering.
- Let the children help with the song service.
- If there is any work being done by someone at the church, if it is not dangerous in any way or risking a breech in confidentiality, then let children help.

Initiative vs. Guilt
- Train your leaders to take this age group seriously. If a child comes and initiates a conversation, honor that and have the conversation. If they start doing something to bless the church, whether it be trying a new ministry or trying to do something nice for others, come along side them and help their efforts. Don't take it over, but

be their assistant.
- From the pulpit praise young people, or old for that matter, who initiate something. Let that be a shining moment for them and the church.

Industry vs. Inferiority
- Have people, even young people, apply for church positions with resume and all. This may seem counterintuitive since we traditionally have a hard time filling positions. But many people feel that if the job is not important enough to vet the candidate, then it is not important enough for them to do.
- Hold people accountable. If people are not doing their job, even if it's a volunteer position, remove them from that role.
- Provide written job descriptions.
- Work hard to create an overall atmosphere that values hard work.
- Use various tools to help young people begin to see what their strengths and weaknesses are, and help them understand that they are uniquely made with these strengths and weaknesses. Some types of tools you may want to use include multiple intelligence inventories, personality inventories, and spiritual gift inventories.

Identity vs. Diffusion
- Have a mentorship program that gives young people an older person who can walk life with them, who can be their sounding board for their ideas and thoughts and be their example.
- Create an atmosphere in your church where people can ask the hard, even blasphemous questions. If it bothers them, they should be able to talk about it without being judged.
- Have sermons and activities designed to help them determine their identity.
- Focus less on the worldly forms of identity (your college, your career, your family) and help them to see their identity as a creation of God, and how they were designed to reflect specific aspects of His character.

Relationship vs. Isolation
- Make sure you have a fellowship meal every single week no matter what. And make sure this meal has the highest quality food, in a

relaxed and pleasant environment (please, don't do it in the dingy basement of your church!), and is an event that people want to stay at for the conversation and activities. It should be like Thanksgiving every week!
- Plan outreach activities that will require people to work together and bond.
- Have family game nights.
- Do crazy events like bowling frozen turkeys or cooking challenges. See Appendix D for more ideas of this nature.
- Make your events the types of events that will be beneficial to your age group.

Appendix D

Fellowship Activities

The following list is just a small taste of what a church family can do together. Sometimes having controlled hang-time events is good, but you may find that just providing opportunities for natural friendships to occur is even better. Either way, here are some ideas to get you started.

- **Have a Weekly Potluck:** Most people bond well over food. That's why couples go out dinner for dates. Having a weekly fellowship meal at church is a good way to break the ice with new people and a great way for the church family to stay connected. If your church is too large to have a fellowship meal, then explore alternatives, like encouraging different families to trade off having meals together at their homes.
- **Rock-A-Thon:** Choose a worthy cause and have sponsors give money for every hour someone rocks in a rocking chair.
- **Paint Ball/Laser Tag:** Be smart. In some circles, this is a no-no. It's also a no-no to do something you know your constituency would be totally against.
- **Cooking Challenge:** Have a contest to see which group can make the best-themed meal in limited time with limited ingredients or cash.
- **Turkey Bowling:** Have a bowling contest in which you replace the ball and pins with a frozen turkey and two-liter soda bottles (or a frozen chicken breast and little juice bottles for little kids).
- **Game Show Night:** Family Feud, The Pyramid, Fear Factor, and other such games can be a real blast.
- **Geocaching:** Look it up online. There are probably sites near you!
- **Great Race:** Come up with crazy things for contestants to do. Examples would be to find a train caboose or have a stranger feed you a candy bar while you do a handstand. Every crazy item is worth a certain amount of points. Drive around your town in groups getting photographic evidence of what you have completed from the list. Rejoin and show your pictures, have laughs, earn a trophy, and

enjoy some pizza and a movie.
- **Join Hobby Groups:** Be real. Be authentic. Be friends. Be Christians. Have fun.
- **Have A Mini-Golf Tournament**
- **Have A Foosball Tournament**
- **Have Any Kind of Tournament**
- **Movie Night**
- *Just Get Together And Have Fun! Do What Friends Do!*

Appendix E

Service Activities

One of the great things about service is that, like fellowship, it is a natural builder of friendships. The following list is a small sampling of what a church family can do together to connect to each other and to connect with their community.

- Paint a House: Just be safe with the ladders and other equipment. Check with laws in your state and your insurance company to see if there are regulations regarding who can be on a ladder.
- Landscaping: Anything from simple weeding to a "yard remodel job."
- Work With Other Organizations: We used to team up with the Lion's Club in our area and waited tables for their pancake breakfasts on Super Bowl Sunday. We didn't have to purchase anything; we didn't have to set up, or tear down, or clean up. We just had to show up, make connections with the community through serving them food, and raise some money for a good cause in the process.
- Adopt A Grandparent: They may be in a nursing home, or they may be in their own home, but many elderly people are lonely and truly need help doing things they cannot do on their own. A regular visit to these people, whether or not chores are done, can just make their day (and yours too!). If you re working with a group of young (or not-so-young) children, helping them to cultivate a relationship with an older person can be an experience, they may not get in today's world anymore. The psychological and developmental blessings for those kids cannot be put easily into words.
- Mission Trips: Nothing says "service" like a mission trip. This can be overseas, within the country, and even locally in your hometown. It can be big or small, but it is always a great experience.
- Clean A Park/Road/Sidewalk: This may not seem like much, but I have had people bring my crew food, drinks, and treats (as in food that tastes too good to be healthy for you) due to their immense gratitude that someone actually cared to do this basic task.

- Rake Leaves/Shovel Snow: A classic example of community service that never gets old, especially for those unable to do it themselves (they may even make you cookies!).
- Host A Family Or Community Game Night: This may not seem like service, but sometimes in today's society our communities just need a safe and enjoyable place to be. A family game night at your church or facility may be just what they need.
- Make-You-Smile Ministry: Just go out and find goofy ways to make people smile. You can give high fives, or walk invisible dogs, or do flash mobs, or anything else that will create a shared memory for others and bring a smile to their face. What a service!
- Give Fire Wood To Those Who Heat With It: Keeping people warm in the winter is a great service and one that will be remembered for a long time. One of the churches in our area does this every year.

Appendix F

Interactive Bible Study Ideas And Resources

When doing an interactive group Bible study, especially if youth are involved, it is important to keep in mind the following four things:

- Youth want to study the Bible (so do adults!). They don't want to be told the same things over and over again but want to explore it and make it their own.
- Youth need to be in the Bible with their peers (and if they are strong in the interpersonal intelligence, so do adults!). Their peers are typically the most important people in their lives, and they need this group to travel in the Bible with them, together.
- Youth desire mentoring (so do adults, especially if they're new Christians!). They don't want to be told what to do or what not to do. They want to be guided in how they can make apply the Bible their lives and walk the Christian walk.
- Youth must be engaged (do you know any adults that don't?). To simply lecture is to simply disengage them. They must be engaged through multiple senses and activities, and yet be left to feel that what they are doing is somehow childish.

In the table below is a model of how you can construct an engaging youth Bible study that will fulfill the requirements above. This is only a model, and it is a flexible one, so feel free to change it and mold it to meet the needs of your youth.

Model Format	Model Format with Model Details

I. Attention Getter/Ice Breaker
II. Introduction of Scripture Video
III. Video
IV. Small Group Discussion
V. Activity
VI. Whole Group Discussion
VII. Challenge
	I. **Attention Getter/Ice Breaker**
	a. Ping Pong Cup Challenge (see below in Resources)
	II. **Introduction of Scripture**
	a. John 11:38-45
	b. Break youth into small groups. Assign each group a verse and ask them to come up with a creative method of sharing it.
	III. **Video**
	a. Skit Guys Video on Lazarus
	b. https://www.youtube.com/watch?v=F9yIM5G9QM8
	IV. **Small Group Discussion**
	a. They will discuss in the small groups formed above.
	b. Questions will include:
	  i. How is Christ's humanity seen in this story?
	  ii. How is Christ's divinity seen in this story?
	  iii. Is there any tension between His divinity and humanity?
	  iv. What does this mean for us?
	c. Method of discussion:
	  i. Jigsaw Puzzle (see description below in Resources)
	V. **Activity**
	a. Titanic: Use a hula-hoop to simulate a porthole on the Titanic. We need to get everyone through without leaving anyone behind. They have to figure out how to do it.
	b. In this life, we all will feel

like we're sinking in suffering and grief. How can we get each other through it?

VI. **Whole Group Discussion**
   a. Situational discussion:
      i. How can the knowledge we gain of Jesus' divinity and humanity in this story help us know how to relate to suffering in our world today? What limitations do we have that He didn't, and how does that affect our ability to relate to suffering?

VII. **Challenge**
   a. Be Christ's representatives to alleviate suffering in your sphere.
   b. The challenge may change/broaden/become more specific depending on the direction of the discussion.

Resources

This is not meant to be an exhaustive list of resources. Rather, here are some quick ideas you can use to improve youth Bible study in a short amount of time.

Attention Getters/Ice Breakers/Activities
- **Ping Pong Cup Challenge:** Material needed is two Dixie Cups and one Ping-Pong Ball. Can anyone get the ball from one ball to the next without touching the ball, squeezing the cup, or tossing the ball from one cup to the next? Secret: Blow across the top of the cup. The ball will lift out.
- **Mousetrap Trust Walk:** Set a number of mousetraps and space them throughout the room. The youth are broken into pairs. One needs to walk barefoot, and blindfolded/eyes shut through the mousetraps while their partner verbally gives them directions. Switch roles.

- **Trust Falls**
- **Ping Pong Cup Challenge 2:** Materials needed are masking tape, paper/plastic cups, and Ping-Pong balls. Place cup on the ground, opening up, against a wall. Pick a distance away from the wall between 3 and 6 feet away from the cups. Youth stand behind the line and try to toss the ball into the cup.
- **Books of Activities:**
    - Silver Bullets
    - 300 + Sizzling Icebreakers
    - Awesome Icebreakers
    - Teen Talk in a Jar

Method for Introducing Scripture

- Creative Readings: Break youth into groups and have them develop creative ways to read the passage.
- Assign A Person To Read: Sometimes keeping it simple is good. Assign a person to read the verse/passage in advance, so there is no awkwardness in waiting for volunteers. This works best with brief readings.
- Word Shout: Before reading the passage, identify 1-3 words that will be in the passage. When the words come up in the reading, the youth need to shout or somehow emphasize those words.
- Word Shout 2: Have papers taped under their chairs. Before reading the passage, everyone looks under the chairs to see if they have a paper. If they do, they are responsible for shouting or emphasizing their specific word. The whole passage can be divided up, or just specific words.

Videos

- The Skit Guys provide many excellent video choices. A partial list of good videos from this source is as follows:
    - https://www.youtube.com/watch?v=F9yIM5G9QM8
    - https://www.youtube.com/watch?v=hB7kev_n4SU
    - https://www.youtube.com/watch?v=hT93Yv1PuJs
    - https://www.youtube.com/watch?v=5fojfRjh4Ac
    - https://www.youtube.com/watch?v=wlTzgTW3WaE
    - https://www.youtube.com/watch?v=ilnn_3PN1VE
    - https://www.youtube.com/watch?v=TPhxByH_xtw
    - https://www.youtube.com/watch?v=zkprjeipGD4

- Blue Fish TV
    - https://www.youtube.com/watch?v=Pv9MRjt2e9I
    - https://www.youtube.com/watch?v=gEftDn-OOUY
    - https://www.youtube.com/watch?v=07kXYl5eMxI
    - https://www.youtube.com/watch?v=-j34Uwgw5Zs
    - https://www.youtube.com/watch?v=efI-spY4vZ0
    - https://www.youtube.com/watch?v=ad-Dm0Ac9rA

Small/Whole Group Discussion Techniques and Resources

- **Jig Saw Puzzle:** This strategy is used to discuss a topic with multiple points. The youth are divided into groups, and each group will ultimately discuss all the points in the topic. Prior to that final discussion, each person in the group is assigned one of the discussion points. Then the groups are split up, and all members from the different groups that have been assigned a topic will meet. In this way, new groups are formed to discuss the specific discussion topics. After a time the members return to their original group, and each member is now a "specialist" in their specific topic. The original groups now discuss all the topics with insights from their "specialists," and prepare to share with the entire youth group their views on the topics.
- **Think-Pair-Share:** This strategy is used when there are youth members who don't typically share or are shy. A discussion topic is posed. Each individual thinks about their views on the topic silently in their heads. Then they discuss their views with a partner. Then the partners share with the group.
- **Continuum Line:** This strategy is used when an opinion question or a moral dilemma is the topic of discussion. The question is posed, and the youth are asked to make a decision as to where they stand on that topic. Literally, they will stand. One end of the room represents one side of the topic, and the other end of the room is the polar opposite side of the topic. The youth will stand somewhere in the room to show where they stand in relation to this topic. Opportunities can be offered for them to discuss with the group as a whole, or in small groups, or in pairs the reason for their stance.
- **Four Corners:** This strategy is similar to the continuum line above, but is used when there is more than one potential answer to the topic. In this scenario, each corner of the room represents a potential stand on the topic, and the young people take their stand in the

room relative to their views. Discussion can proceed in a fashion similar to the Continuum Line.

- **Say and Switch:** This strategy is used when there may be a need for two people, or groups of two people, to learn how to discuss opposite sides of a topic and try to see the other person's perspective. In advance, the facilitator/leader prepares two cards for the two individuals in the group(s). Each person has questions on their card to ask the other. Person one asks a question, and person two responds. Then person two asks a question, and person one responds. Repeat this until all questions are answered. Then the cards are switched so that the participants are switching roles, and they repeat the process.

Appendix G

Training Your Ministry Team For Connections

The key for this section is that, while there are many ways to organize a ministry team, you must, and I mean must be purposeful in maintaining a commitment to connection. Organization for organization's sake is not good enough. Organization to improve the quality and quantity of connections you can make as a leader to those you are ministering to is the goal.

- Organize your elders/ministerial team so that they each oversee/support a department/ministry of the church and reports back to the board of elders/ministerial team.
- Have church members rotate the teaching of the main class so that the pastor can rotate through all the classes.
- Have a committee that develops and runs family-friendly events, with the pastor's only responsibility to connect with people at the event.
- Smaller churches that don't have the numbers to create a ministerial team should just make every member a team. They should focus on making family-like connections among all members, and then plan on how to maintain this when the church grows.
- Develop a method by which you and your ministry team can learn the name of every member and regular visitor of your church.
- Don't rely on the guestbook method to make connections with visitors. Develop a way for your team to quickly make connections with visitors, learning their names on the spot, and finding ways to connect with them while they are there. Waiting to make connections in a follow-up meeting is a mistake; that meeting may never happen.
- Use some sort of background check for your ministry team and anyone working with young people.
- Use some sort of training with your ministry team and anyone working as a mentor that will include not only mentoring strategies but also training on avoiding (as in not committing), identifying, and properly dealing with abuse.

- Develop with your ministry team a system that will help them identify people in need of mentoring and potential mentors.

Appendix H

Model Sermon Format

Please understand, this is a model sermon format. There is no such thing as a perfect model or a one-size-fits-all formula. This is just one idea for you to add to your tool box, to get your creative preaching juices flowing, and to help you try to connect in a way you may not have been previously able to do. In your own practice, please feel free to add to it, chop things out of it, change the order, change the time for each section, or do anything else that will help you be successful. In other words, this is just a suggestion, not a commandment written in stone.

This model is based on the philosophy we have at B.A.C., where we believe in shorter sermons that get straight to the point. We don't lack "meat," we just get rid of the "fluff." We also try to make it connect to many multiple intelligences, and we encourage interaction throughout the whole sermon.

I. Visual Aid (5 min)
II. Tie Into One Scripture (3 min)
III. Story (2 min)
IV. Summarize Point (5 min)
V. Small Group Discussion (5 min)
VI. Closing Prayer

About the Author

Jeremy Garlock, MA, is currently working as the Education Director and Associate Youth Director for the New York Conference of Seventh-day Adventists, and Earned his MA in Leadership. He has been a teacher at several small church schools, where he was heavily involved in helping to grow and changes programs to be more effective at reaching young people for Jesus. Jeremy has also been a church planter, camp pastor, and youth leader.

The pride of Jeremy's life is his wonderful family, which includes his wife Joya, and four children, Rilla, Brook, Marissa, and Kai. They help him remember every day how much he really doesn't know about all things he claims to know.

Contact Jeremy at JeremyGarlock@gmail.com.

www.ingramcontent.com/pod-product-compliance
Lightning Source LLC
Chambersburg PA
CBHW051700090426
42736CB00013B/2459